MW00914099

THE PROBLEM WITH MEN

by Kelli Giammarco, Debra Keller, Margaret Lannamann, and Karen Tom

ISBN: 0-7407-3350-8

02 03 04 05 06 BID 10 9 8 7 6 5 4 3 2 1

Library of Congress Catalog Card Number: 2002111555

Book designed by Junie Lee Tait

THE PROBLEM WITH MEN

INTRODUCTION

The Problem with Men Is . . .
They Are Not Women.

Men—we love them, we can't live without them—but life would certainly be easier if they could act more like us! Their behavior can easily exasperate the most even-tempered woman. One minute they're all puffed up and running the show, and the next minute they're as helpless as a baby. One minute they're focused on romance and sweet conversation, and the next minute they're surfing the channels looking for football. The men in our lives, whether they're boyfriends, husbands, friends, or coworkers, can be annoying, immature, and unreliable, but there's no doubt about it, they make wonderful targets for a woman's sense of humor!

Defying Gravity

The basic laws of gravity do not apply with men. A toilet seat that goes up does not come down.

Sick Day

Lying in bed needing hot soup and constant attention is an act reserved for men only. Women's colds are *never* that bad.

What Single Men Really Mean . . .

When He Says	**What He Means Is**
Nice dress.	I'd like to have sex with you.
Can I call you?	I'd like to have sex with you.
I'm hungry.	I'd like to have sex with you.
I'm tired.	Do you want to have sex now?
I love you.	Let's have sex now.
I'll call you.	I want to have sex with some-one else now.

Can I Have Your Attention, Please?

If you want to get his immediate attention,
hide the remote control.

The Four Ages of Man

1. childhood
2. puberty
3. adolescence

Qualified Applicants Only!

Men think turning eighteen and having a
penis are the only qualifications that make
them men.

Locked Out

No matter how many times you suggest
calling roadside assistance, he'll use that
coat hanger until hypothermia sets in.

Mr. Fix It

Before a man calls a repair shop he must first disassemble the appliance and attempt to fix it himself, thus ensuring a repair bill worth bragging about.

←

It's Not *That* Full

To a man, stuffing the garbage into the over-flowing garbage can seem more practical than just taking it out.

A Penny for His Thoughts

You don't need a crystal ball to know what a man is thinking about. It will either be food or sex. Any other thought is just fleeting.

Mother's Day

Don't expect a man to buy his mom a Mother's Day gift. Whatever you get your mom will do just fine for his.

The Ten Commandments of Manhood

1 You shall worship no other but yourself.

2 You shall idolize the *Victoria's Secret* catalog.

3 You shall not speak the name of any sports channel except with reverence.

4 You shall keep every day as a day of rest.

5 You shall show no respect to your wife's mother and father.

6 You shall commit indecent acts in public.

7 You shall at least be unfaithful in your heart.

8 You shall steal food off everyone else's plate.

9 You shall speak falsely about love and commitment.

10 You shall covet all other men's women.

Maps, What Are They Good For?

Men think that maps simply do not work.

Equal Opportunity Housework

The modern man's approach to sharing housework: You do the shopping, cooking, cleaning, gardening, and laundry and he'll do all the rest.

If a Tree Falls in the Woods . . .

If a man is alone in a rest room does he still wash his hands when he's done?

Gone Fishin'

Only men could've dreamt up a sport where
they spend all day sitting around trying
to lodge a sharp metal object into a
fish's mouth.

More of Him to Love

Men truly believe love handles are lovable.

Mirror Image

Mirrors, computer monitors, shiny car hoods. When there's no one else around to adore him, his reflection will do just fine.

Honey, How Do I Look?

If you ask a man how you look, the answer will always be "fine." The shoes you're wearing look fine, the dress you're wearing looks fine, your hair looks fine, your nails look fine, and the dress you were wearing ten minutes ago looked fine too.

Under the Hood

To the average man, solving car problems is a three-step process:

1. pop the hood
2. stare at the engine intently until another man arrives
3. crack open a beer

Attention Grabber

If you change your hair or buy a
new blouse, don't expect him to notice.
But if you move the beer to a different
shelf in the refrigerator . . .

Maturity

The primary difference between a man and a melon is that a melon eventually matures.

Star Struck

Men consider going to movies starring Arnold Schwarzenegger or Jean-Claude Van Damme to be cultural experiences.

Lights Out

How many men does it take to change a light-bulb? None. It's only women who notice things that need fixing around the house.

Looking for Love

If a married woman wants love, romance, and affection she should get a divorce.

Toeing the Line

Why is it that men need to be
reminded to cut their toenails?

Hero

All men are heroes . . . in their own
minds, anyway.

Bad Things

Inside a man's head, commitment is like castration—an all-around bad, scary, and unnecessary act.

Vanity

Sure men are vain, but they must also be delusional. What else could explain the popularity of the comb-over hairstyle?

Tears of Fear

The problem with men is they think
that crying shrinks their penises.

Beer

Men and beer are a lot alike. Their only value is in their body; above the neck they're nothing but air.

Something to Bank On

If you want security and a little interest, get a savings account.

What's That Smell?

Men have not figured out that the scents of heavy sweat, oil, dirt, or grease do not turn women on.

Periscope Vision

If a man's in his garage and the TV's on inside, he will still claim to be watching it.

The Language of Flowers

If men want women to actually believe that their gift of flowers is a romantic act of love and devotion they should stop buying them at the grocery store.

Après Sex

When you feel the need to speak your mind,
wait until after sex; that way he can't argue
back. He'll be asleep.

Companionship

If you feel yourself getting interested in finding a man, stop—and think about adopting a pet instead.

Turn It On, Baby

Two ways to get a man to listen to you:
1. show a little leg
2. disguise yourself as a stereo

Underwear

Next time you're embarrassed by your husband prancing around the front yard in his underwear, remember this: Everyone else's husband does it too.

So Many Confusing Buttons

When it comes to electronics, men somehow have an amazing ability to wire the complete house with just several extension cords and aluminum foil. However, when it comes to using the washing machine or vacuum, technophobia sets in.

Efficiency

Single guys can be models of efficiency.
Consider their kitchen sinks—they're
simultaneously sinks, cupboards, trash cans,
and, on occasion, microbreweries.

Advice for the Mother-to-Be

No need to worry about how you will handle your children; just handle them the same way you handle your husband. There's not that much difference between them.

Commitment

Q. What mammal has a highly developed brain *and* mates for life?

A. A whale.

Envy

As any man will tell you, it's not women who experience penis envy—it's all the other guys in the locker room.

Death Notice

It is quite reasonable, after your man spends an entire weekend on the sofa watching sports on TV, to have him declared legally dead.

Noise Please

Men are comforted by things that make noise: engines, power tools, televisions, stereos. If none of those are easily accessible, their own bodily functions will do just fine.

Laying It on the Line

When a man has sex, he gets laid. When a woman has sex, she gets screwed.

Smart Shoppers

Why should a man purchase a $100 telescope he only plans on using once when he can purchase a $1,000 telescope he only plans on using once? Smart shoppers know that when it comes to impressing your buddies, money talks.

What Men Know

The three most important things enlightened men have learned about women:

1.

2.

3.

Ex-Boyfriends

Ex-boyfriends make excellent speed bumps.

The Nose Knows

To a man's way of thinking, why wash your socks if you can't smell them with your shoes on?

Emotion

It's not true that men don't show their emotions. Tell him his favorite NFL coach has been fired and you'll see some emotion.

61

Lawn Chairs

You can tell a man's marital status by what he does with a lawn chair. If he carries one with him at all times no matter how embarrassing or inappropriate, it's likely he's someone's husband. If he sets one up in his living room, it's likely he's not.

TV Dining

To the average man, the term "TV dinner" is a redundancy.

Hunting

The reason more men go hunting than women is because they have an intrinsic need to outwit creatures who are smarter than themselves.

Retail Therapy

The problem with men is that they don't under-
stand that shopping is an art. One that
requires many years to perfect.

Best Friends

If dogs are a man's best friend and diamonds are a girl's best friend, it's easy to determine which sex is smarter.

Tools

Men collect tools the way squirrels gather nuts. It's their instinct to hoard them, save them for a rainy day, and sometimes forget where they're buried, but if you find them first and move them they will bite.

Girlfriends

Nothing makes you appreciate your girl-
friends more than a romantic weekend away
with your man.

Problems

Men are the root of most women's
problems: *men*struation, *men*opause,
*men*tal breakdown . . .

Men's Equation for Measuring Masculinity

Beer consumption = Brawn

Like Fine Wine

The maturation process for men and wine is pretty much the same: You pick the ones that show the most promise and keep them in the dark until they develop, and they just might turn into something you'd like to have dinner with.

Safekeeping

If you want to keep your boyfriend from reading your journal, store it in a box labeled "Operating Instructions."

Birth Control

If men were the ones who gave birth to babies, the population of the world would be considerably lower.

Bigger, Better, Best

Everything a man owns must be bigger, better, and more expensive than his neighbor's.

The Tenets of Men

Three beliefs common among men:

1. A little hypochondria never hurt anyone
2. When in doubt, have a beer
3. Rest today—tomorrow you may be dead

Animal Instincts

It's not just the month of March that comes like a lion and leaves like a lamb.

Deep Thoughts

The first thing a man thinks of when he sees a beautiful sunset is who might win the playoffs this year.

Whistle While You Work

The reason why men whistle all the time is to fool themselves into believing they're doing something.

Bathroom Annoyances

It's a simple concept but it gets men all the time: After you've used up the toilet paper, put a new roll on the holder.

The Hidden Language of Men

Like most animal species, men have an unspoken language. When they slap each other on their backs, shake hands, or give high fives what they're really saying is, "May you keep your stomach full and your testicles empty."

Environmentally Friendly

Keeping a man around the house is a handy way to cut down on kitchen waste.

Are You Listening to Me?

As far as making the distinction between hearing and listening—well, men have yet to discover that there *is* a distinction.

Above the Glass Ceiling

The only reason men let women break through the glass ceiling is so they can stand below and look up their skirts.

The Perfect Gift

When you can't think of anything else to get the man in your life, try a global positioning system. He can use it while lying on the couch all day to make sure he hasn't moved.

Too Many Numbers to Remember

It's not a problem for men to store sports statistics (who hit the most RBIs last year) or team information (the name of every NFL defensive coordinator) in their heads, but remembering their anniversary can baffle their precious little minds.

Nuptial Diet

If you want to lose weight, get married. There isn't a husband alive who doesn't pick food off his wife's plate.

Family Vacation

If you want your kids to wear clothes that match, don't let Dad pack their suitcases.

Hair So Soft

Men love to run their hands through soft, silky curls, especially those that sprout from their own chests.

Perfection

There is only one perfect man in the world and every wife has to put up with him.

Handymen

Marry a man who's handy. That way he'll be too busy puttering around the house to get on your nerves.

The Mark of Man

It's a man's nature to splash outside the toilet bowl; since he no longer lives in a cave, it's his only means of marking his territory.

Tell Me Another One

Men love to carry on fantasies in their head. For example, they think they are the dominant sex.

Gold Medal Effort

At the rate men perform exercises in futility
you'd think it was an Olympic sport.

Eye Contact

The reason so few women see eye to eye with men is because most men are focused on women's chests.

Dirt = Work

Men think that the dirtier they can get, the
more productive they have been.

On the Run

Men, like mascara, tend to run when
tears flow.

Driving You Crazy

You can usually tell how a man feels about
the event he's attending by the speed at
which he's driving to it.

Light My Fire

Contrary to some men's beliefs, turning off the lights does *not* constitute foreplay.

Napkins

It doesn't matter how big the napkin in his lap is, the edge of the tablecloth will always be better.

Meat Me at the Buffet

An overwhelming percentage of men only recognize one food group—meat, which includes nuts and beer.

The Perfect Spot

It doesn't matter how many parking spaces there are a block from the restaurant. If there's not one right in front he'll keep circling until he finds one, like a vulture waiting for the kill.

Forever Mine

The only person a man remains deeply in love with for all eternity is himself.

Fishermen

Of course more men than women fish—men are better at standing around doing nothing.

Homework

A man's idea of helping his kids with homework is muting the commercials to give them a little quiet time.

Cooking 101

Contrary to what a man might believe, knowing how to operate a toaster oven does not mean one knows how to cook.

A Mind Like a Sieve

The average man can remember the score of
every football game played in his lifetime
but the only birthday he can remember is
his own.

Window-Shopping

Like pretty things displayed in store windows, men tend to be more appealing *before* you bring them home.

Droppings

No wonder men drop their dirty clothes on the floor and leave them there until a woman picks them up. Seems like just yesterday they were doing the same thing with toys tossed out of their cribs.

Modeling Clay

Husbands are like a lump of clay. It takes
patience and skill to mold them into something desirable.

The Working Man

When you ask him to watch the kids and take out the garbage, expect to see skid marks on the kitchen floor.

Emotional Insight

Men think, "I'm fine, thanks," is being open
with how they feel.

Diamonds or Furs or Jewelry . . .

Why is it that men just don't get it that vacuum cleaners simply do not make good birthday gifts?

Stand-Ins

Men never seem to be embarrassed asking a female shopper to stand in for their absent wife or girlfriend, but they should be. Not because they asked, but because of what it is they're considering buying.

Cuddle Time

If a woman wants to sleep with something soft, comforting, and reliable she should try a teddy bear.

Ego Feeding

If you want to seem like a brilliant conversationalist in your man's eyes, forget the arts, forget politics, and just talk about *him*.

Marriage

Men are the reason marriage is called an "institution."

Pedicure

To a man's way of thinking, why shell out
$1.49 for a pair of toenail clippers when he
already has a perfectly good set of teeth?

Four Things to Look for in a Man

1. Sensitivity
2. The ability to communicate
3. A good sense of humor
4. Vasectomy scars

An Offer He Can't Refuse

There *is* a way for a woman to get what she wants from a man. It's called blackmail.

Breathe In . . .

Men must be under the mistaken impression that all women are nearsighted. They somehow believe that taking a deep breath will obscure the four inches of gut hanging over the edge of their pants.

Never Say No

The only woman a man can never say no to
is his mother.

Multitasking

The typical man can watch fourteen channels at the same time but if you ask him to do two things at once it's so stressful he has to stop and go have a beer.

Chivalry

Chivalry exists only when someone else is watching.

Listen Here

If you want to communicate with a man, replace the TV remote with a walkie-talkie.

What We Wish For

Women want to be trusted, needed, and loved. Men want . . . tickets to the Super Bowl.

Cock-a-Doodle-Do!

Remember: No matter how loudly a rooster crows it's only the hen who's productive.

Usefulness

It's a good idea to keep a man around the house in case you ever need that cast iron skillet you keep in the back of the top shelf of the kitchen cupboard. And if you don't ever need it, he might just give you a reason.

Like What You've Done with the Place

As for home décor, thumbtacks, magazines,
and a recliner are all most men need to
do the job.

Not His

Men do not own hair dryers. If you find one in a man's bathroom it is not his. It never was and it never will be. It might have been left there by a former girlfriend or his mother or the maid and he is only using it to keep the motor primed until its rightful owner comes to claim it.

Backseat Driver

Men hate to be told that their driving is less than perfect. But when they plow into the back of a parked car, it's always your fault for not warning them.

Fill 'er Up

If you want him to stop at the grocery store, tell him they're giving away free samples.

Kitchen Genius

The average man is a genius of economy when it comes to cooking. The only utensil he needs is a can opener.

Mr. Manners

The lower you set your expectations, the happier you'll be.

Fatal Attraction

All it takes is one woman to tell a man he's attractive for him to believe he's God's gift to all women. It might have been his old Aunt Peg with the two-inch cataracts when he was seven years old, but it was enough.

Boyfriends and Husbands

The most boring boyfriends make the best husbands. They've had the most practice.

Fowl Play

Don't get mad, get even. Line the bird cage with the sports section before he reads it.

Good Advice

The most important thing to look for in
Mr. Right is a pulse.

Good Fortune

If a woman hasn't met the right man by the time she's thirty . . . she should count her lucky stars.

Superhero!

Even grown-up men play superhero—fighting the battle between good and evil and taming the flames of doom—when flipping burgers on a barbecue.

Time to Yourself

When you need to be alone, head for the laundry. It's the one room he doesn't know exists.

The Perfect Man

The Tooth Fairy, Santa Claus, and The Perfect Man are all cut from the same cloth.

Food for Thought

To men, food always tastes better when it's off someone else's plate.

The One That Got Away

That was no ordinary undersized trout he had to release. That was an undersized trout caught with a $1,800 rod and a $75 fly.

Etiquette

It's not true that men don't know how to use forks. As most men know, forks make excellent catapults for peas and other small vegetables.

Quiet Evening

If you want a nice, quiet dinner out, suggest a restaurant with a TV.

Hair, There, and Everywhere

It's a Pavlovian response: The minute a man sees the glistening basin of the just-cleaned bathroom sink he feels compelled to trim his mustache.

TLC

If your upset stomach is bad enough, a good man just might take care of you. Never mind how his tuna fish omelet topped with a dollop of mayonnaise might make you feel, it's the thought that counts.

Cold Front

Men are like the weather—unpredictable and constantly changing.

Battle Scars

If a man has a scar, he'll wear it like a badge of honor. Never mind that he got it from falling off the "Caution: this is not a step" rung of a ladder—that part of the story is irrelevant.

Fly Away

A man can be a lot like a fly—he swarms around food, annoys you in the kitchen, and is next to impossible to get rid of. But the minute you try to catch him, he darts away.

Armchair Quarterback

Men think *watching* sports is the same as actually *playing* them.

Indirectly Speaking

HOW A MAN MIGHT TELL ANOTHER MAN
HIS FLY IS DOWN:

"Your Ford's poking out of your garage."

"Your pickle's leaving the deli."

"There's a hull breach on your lower deck."

"You need to bring your tray table to the
upright and locked position."

Directly Speaking

HOW A WOMAN MIGHT TELL ANOTHER
WOMAN HER FLY IS DOWN:
"Your fly is down."

Looking Good

If you want a man to look his best, take him to a beach full of young women in bikinis.

Thermostat Wars

There are only two ways to keep the temperature where you like it: Live alone or break the thermostat.

Strive for Mediocrity

The only way he can be good at everything is
if everything he does is mediocre.

Reach for the Stars

Any woman who strives to be on an equal
footing with men lacks ambition.

Pork Chop Torture

If you want to drive a man crazy, invite his best friend to dinner but only make one extra pork chop.

Someone Should Tell Them

Men need to know the truth: Armpit farts are
only funny if you're twelve.

However . . .

Men can be irresistibly cute at times, and one can't help but accept all their shortcomings and love them anyway.